T OUSAND
YEARS

Stephen Conlin

THE O'BRIEN PRESS
DUBLIN

Dubh Linn · Baile Atha Cliath · Dublin

Dublin has always been a port of entry to Ireland for strangers and exotic goods, as much in the far distant past as today. From the first silks that arrived in Viking times up to the latest 'high-tech' advances, Dublin has communicated with the rest of the world on a level that has often bewildered and alienated the rest of the country.

The Vikings built their town on a road junction near the sea, a site suitable for trade and limited settlement; having arrived as obvious foreigners, they mixed with the native Irish to the extent that Hiberno-Norse is an acceptable way of describing them. The Normans came with the hope of subjugating Ireland; but in time many of their leaders became headstrong and independent, in some cases throwing in their lot with the Irish. As Anglo-Norman rule became purely English, Dublin was used as the base for expeditions from the Pale, a ring of castles which encircled the Dublin region. The Tudor conquests were carried out by men who had all the benefits of the highest education available in Europe, yet their sensibilities did not extend to showing mercy to the Gaelic Irish.

With Irish opposition crushed in the seventeenth century, the Protestant Ascendancy was established and Dublin began to develop as an important urban centre of great architectural merit. The buildings of Georgian Dublin provided the backdrop for an elegant social life revolving around parliament and public entertainments. When the Act of Union removed the legislative assembly in 1801, Dublin was deprived of the *raison d'être* of her greatness and went into a decline.

Since independence, some people have seen Dublin's architecture as 'borrowed robes' in which the new state should not be dressed. But the failure to recognise the city's fabric as a national asset could result in major loss for the country as a whole. If we are lucky enough to find archaeological sites of international importance and to own architecture of which any city would be proud, we should see ourselves at the very least as curators whose duty it is to preserve a collection of buildings whose merit has never been in doubt. No city which lacks a history can buy what Dublin possesses as a legacy of the past.

Dublin's reputation abroad rests partly on the literature of the past hundred years, but the tradition of verbal brilliance goes back to Jonathan Swift. If there is one literary giant whose work should confirm that Dublin is worth preserving, it is James Joyce, whose major work *Ulysses* is entirely bound up with the city and its surroundings.

Dublin, A Thousand Years is made up of drawings and commentaries which aim to provide an impression of how Dublin must have looked down through the years. In some instances a well-known site may have changed utterly, in others an important building may be the same, but the city has grown up round it.

Archaeologists and medieval specialists have given freely of their time to provide information on the appearance of Dublin as suggested by the evidence of excavation and limited documentation. Contemporary maps, drawings, engravings and paintings were consulted for the later images, which were commented upon by art historians and other specialists.

The process of drawing began in each case with a perspective study in pencil, which could then be inked up using a fine-line pen to provide a framework in three or four colours. Watercolour then flooded the image and texture was added with coloured pencil. The picture was then 'lit' by shadow projection.

When I first came to live in Dublin as a student in the 1970s, it was one of my greatest pleasures simply to explore the city. I little suspected that I would have the opportunity to express myself so fully as in this publication. Like James Malton and many other topographical artists before and since the eighteenth century, I 'was struck with admiration at the beauty of the capital of Ireland, and was desirous to make a display of it to the World'.

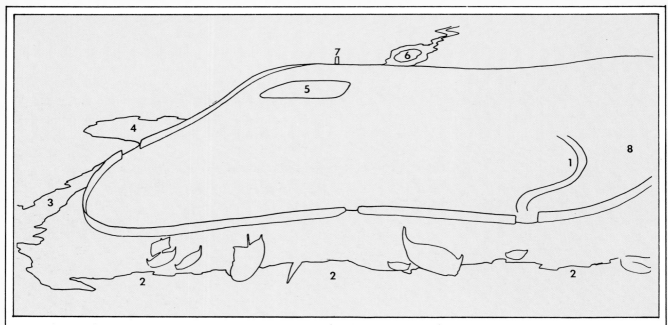

Viking Dublin *circa* 988, looking southwards from above the river Liffey. The pool, centre left, provided safe anchorage and was probably used for refitting and building ships as shown here.

Key
1 Course of modern Fishamble Street
2 River Liffey
3 River Poddle
4 *'Linn dubh'* or black pool, from which Dublin is named
5 First Viking stronghold
6 Site of St Patrick's Cathedral on an island in the river Poddle; previously a Gaelic foundation
7 Part of the tower of St Michael-le-Pole (90ft tall) also a pre-Viking relic
8 Site of modern Civic Offices

The popular image of Vikings as barbarian marauders has in recent decades been dramatically modified by the results of archaeological digs, nowhere more so than in Dublin. These have shown that once the Vikings settled down to build a major centre, they could become rich and influential through international trade. This success they owed particularly to the flat-bottomed longships, shown here, which made it possible to sail both long distances and up comparatively shallow rivers, as far abroad as Newfoundland, Constantinople and Russia. These craft linked the Viking homelands to the colonies in Britain and Ireland, and opened up trade routes across all the then-known world.

The Gaelic Dublin which they took over was an important hub of the ancient road network, as well as providing shelter for ships. The number of churches in the area would indicate the presence of Gaelic settlement, most likely in the vicinity of the ford of wattles, from which the revived name of Dublin 'Baile Atha Cliath' derives. Until 1781 a Gaelic round tower ninety feet high stood next to the river Poddle. In the Dark Ages Ireland's monasteries acted as important guardians of culture and Christianity, embodied in the eighth-century Book of Kells. The missionary zeal of Irish monks is attested to by the presence of ancient streets named after them in cities as distant as Prague and Vienna.

By 988 Dublin was thriving — notice how densely packed the Viking town was, enclosed by its earthen and timber defences. The houses, made of timber planks or wattle, were regular in style. Fires were lit in a central hearth, so smoke would be rising at all seasons. Inside, women carried out their many tasks, including spinning, weaving and cooking. The Vikings consumed much dietary fibre in the form of vegetables and grains. Pork was the most common fleshmeat, but cattle and sheep also were slaughtered for food. Fish could be dried and thus preserved for eating later. Viking women seem to have enjoyed a higher status than in most other contemporary societies, with such privileges as initiating divorce and inheriting property. In the workshops, men plied their trade as bonecarvers, leather merchants and wood-turners. Down on the shore there was always work to be done, loading or unloading the commodities of international trade.

By 988 there had been enough mixing between Viking and Irish in the north Leinster area for Dublin to have acquired shared characteristics, possibly even bilingualism, as may have been the case also in similar centres such as Limerick, Waterford and Wexford. Certainly the Battle of Clontarf in 1014 was no contest simply of Vikings on one side and Irish on the other, but of various alliances of the two, drawn up against forces of similar profile. Later in the century the Battle of Hastings (1066) in England would bring Norman influence nearer to Ireland.

But who were these Normans? It would appear that they were distant cousins of the Dublin Norse, a kinship which would do nothing to deter the Norman-Welsh from joining forces with Dermot MacMurrough, King of Leinster, to conquer Dublin.

Viking longship (detail from page 5).

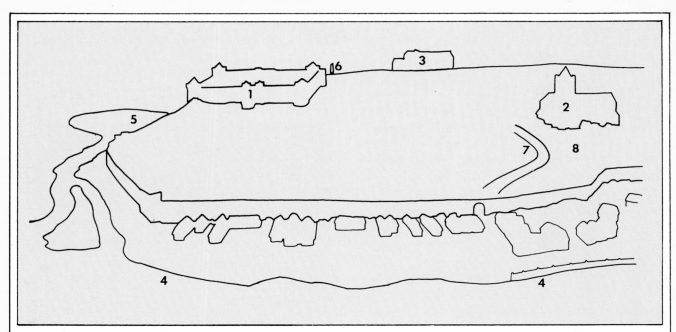

Medieval Dublin *circa* 1275, from the same viewpoint as for the Viking town. Dublin, with its Norman castle and two cathedrals was already a unique centre in Ireland and would have appeared utterly alien to most of the Gaelic-speaking population.

Key
1 Dublin Castle, begun by King John in 1204
2 Cathedral of the Holy Trinity (founded 1038), commonly called Christ Church Cathedral
3 St Patrick's Cathedral (founded 1191), built on low-lying ground outside the town walls
4 Land reclamation creates a new shoreline, particularly at Wood Quay
5 Site of the black pool
6 Tower of St Michael-le-Pole (see Viking Dublin picture)
7 Fishamble Street
8 Site of modern Civic Offices

The Normans were superb warriors and it was as mercenaries that they first arrived in Ireland. One of their leaders, Strongbow, was married to the King of Leinster's daughter, a union which helped to bring about a permanent Anglo-Norman foothold in the country. In 1171 Henry II himself came to Ireland, a visit which links Dublin with his other domains as King of England, Duke of Normandy and Aquitaine and Earl of Anjoû. In 1210 his son, King John, came to Ireland to punish disloyalty amongst wayward and headstrong barons, thereby to consolidate his power. It was King John who ordered the building of Dublin Castle.

In this picture (page 9) the town is densely packed, as in the Viking period, but notice the style of architecture, which has changed to become more sophisticated as a result of Norman influence. Christ Church Cathedral, founded in 1038 by Sitric Silkenbeard probably as a wooden structure, has been rebuilt in stone, and after a century of Norman domination the city has seen some impressive advances in building techniques. In the coming century larger, timber-framed houses of the cage-work type will begin to form the majority. The stone houses scattered throughout the town belong to richer inhabitants and are the forerunners of the many towerhouses which will be built along the city walls. The old Viking wall has been strengthened and built up by the Normans.

On the frozen Liffey shore, land reclamation has been in progress since early in the century, adding considerably to the ground along this stretch. This process will also have the effect of reducing the river breadth whilst increasing its depth and the size of draught possible for shipping. Eventually a second wall, hastily thrown up in 1317 during the threat of conquest by brothers Robert and Edward Bruce of Scotland, will enclose the new quarter. By the time of this view the black pool has become marshy ground, probably the site of the present Castle Garden.

The picture shows roughly ⅔ of the walled town of Dublin in 1275, which also extended westwards, in the direction of St Audoen's parish church, one of the few medieval churches to have survived to the present day. Even some of the old town wall still stands near St Audoen's, giving a glimpse of how medieval Dublin must have looked.

King Henry II's Dublin Charter of 1171/72, which made Dublin into a colony for loyal English subjects.

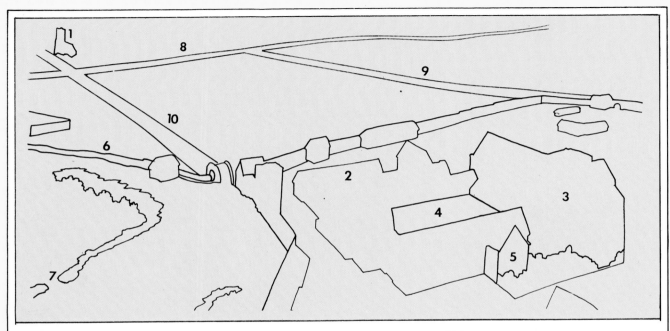

St Mary's Abbey and Oxmanstown *circa* 1450 viewed from above modern Capel Street. This northern suburb was probably quite self-sufficient, with at least four places of worship and its own market.

Key
1 St Michan's Church, later rebuilt in the sixteenth century
2 St Mary's Abbey
3 Church
4 Cloister
5 Chapter house
6 River Bradogue
7 Inlets from the river Liffey

Modern streets
8 **Church Street** leading down to the site of the 'Old Bridge' of Dublin on the site of the present-day Fr Mathew Bridge
9 Mary's Lane
10 Chancery Street

ST MARY'S ABBEY

One of the richest foundations in Ireland, St Mary's was situated on the edge of Dublin, north of the river Liffey. Nearby was Oxmantown, a name derived from Ost- or Eastmen, i.e. Norsemen, who as former inhabitants of Dublin came to live here after being expelled by the Anglo-Normans. This suburb was clustered about the approaches to the Old Bridge of Dublin, the medieval stone bridge which replaced an earlier, perhaps wooden structure in the general area of Ath Cliath, the ford of wattles. When threatened with invasion by the Scottish Bruces in 1317, the citizens of Dublin prepared their defences by demolishing St Saviour's Priory, a Dominican house on the site of the present Four Courts: they carried the stone across the bridge to build a wall along the quays and then destroyed the bridge. Other river crossings nearby were a ferry not far downstream of the bridge and — at low tide only — the possibility of riding over on horseback.

St Mary's Abbey was of the Cistercian order, which usually favoured sites well-removed from centres of population. One of the ideals of the order was simplicity, indeed richness and ornament in everything from architecture to food were forbidden. In spite of this the church building boasted leaden roofing — a sign of wealth — instead of the usual slate or shingle (wooden tiles).

Daily life and its routine varied for the two classes of brethren: the monks, being literate, spent most of their time indoors engaged in clerical work and the recital of church services, whilst the lay brothers worked in the out-buildings and fields. Some impression of these activities is given in the picture on page 13: the monks would have found the cloister useful for communication between cells; within the boundary walls there is beekeeping and tillage, while outside, small boats discharge or take on cargo; the inlets from the river Liffey could have made good fish-traps.

After the Reformation in the sixteenth century St Mary's was dissolved and this area of Dublin seems scarcely to have grown at all until the eighteenth century, when property speculators began to build on ground to the east which was either newly drained or completely reclaimed from the bay. Clues to the abbey's existence are to be found in the Church of Ireland parish of St Mary, in names such as Abbey Street and Mary's Lane, but the most fascinating survival of this site is the Chapter House itself, the interior of which (including the window-openings) was discovered and excavated in 1882. The present street level is eight feet higher than the floor of the Chapter House, as the result of centuries of building, occupation and demolition. It is now in the care of the Board of Works and may be visited by the public, through an entrance from Meeting House Lane.

A typical cog or small medieval ship, which would have been used on the Liffey for trading.

ST PATRICK'S CATHEDRAL

Many medieval cathedrals seem to have served as meeting places, art galleries and even markets. The citizens, seeing the building as an essential part of daily life, did not hesitate to build round and even onto their churches, something which the Victorians seem to have eradicated where possible. Notice that the cathedral, founded in 1191, is surrounded by a suburb of the medieval city and rises to dominate the flat ground which was once an island in the river Poddle. This river, nearing the end of its course, may be glimpsed just to the right of the cathedral's Minot Tower.

On the left beyond the cathedral is the Archbishop's Palace, called St Sepulchre's, a name which dates from the Crusades. This complex of buildings was substantial and at one time hosted the court of law over which the archbishop sat in judgement, and a prison. There are various reports of the palace's neglect down the centuries, but it seems to have been repaired in the 1520s and was occupied by the Lord Deputy under Edward VI. By the 1590s it was described as: 'an agreeable dwelling ... a semi-regal abode well pleasantlie sited as gorgeously builded'.

Today Marsh's Library stands on part of the site, but the actual building can be made out in the fabric of the Garda Station on Kevin Street Upper.

The cathedral has changed little since this period, although it was to suffer neglect and finally be restored in the 1860s by Sir Benjamin Lee Guinness. There is evidence that bells were hung above the crossing, as within the pointed structure here on the roof. The flying buttresses were probably later medieval additions to the thirteenth-century church.

St Patrick's Cathedral *circa* 1500, looking southwards. Even today the Cathedral is an important Dublin landmark but in the medieval period St Patrick's would have dwarfed the dwellings of the people, as was typical in other major European towns and cities. It is still the longest church in Ireland.

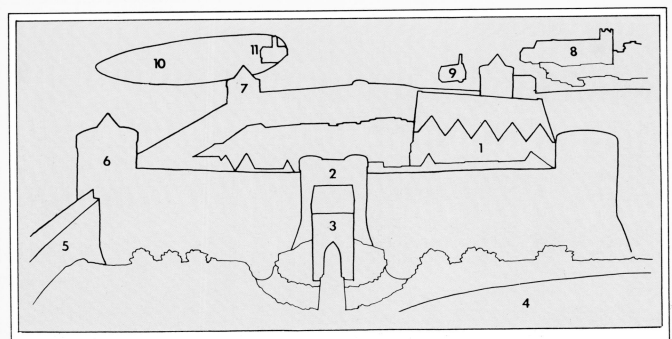

Dublin Castle, 1475, looking southwards — almost completely unrecognisable when compared with the present castle. The only substantial surviving part of this complex is the Record Tower.

Key
1 The Great Hall
2 Castle Gate
3 Barbican
4 Present Castle Street
5 City Wall
6 Storehouse Tower
7 Record Tower (modern name), formerly the Black Tower
8 St Patrick's Cathedral and suburb
9 Church of St Michael-le-Pole
10 Ancient enclosure, still evident in modern street plan
11 St Mary's Priory, a Carmelite house on the site of the present Adelaide Hospital

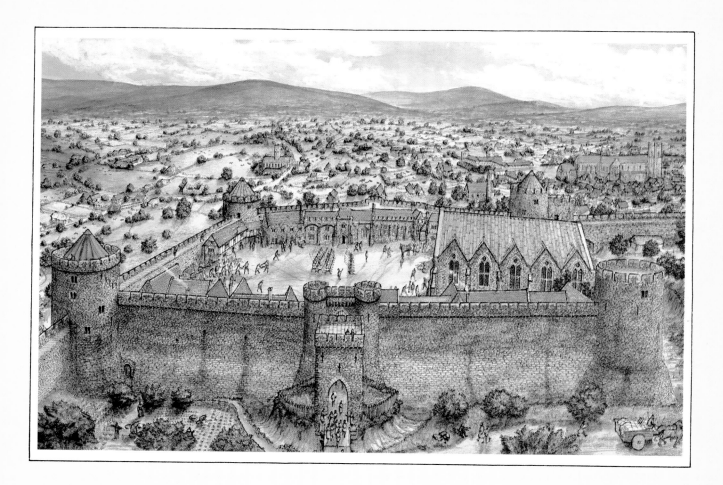

DUBLIN CASTLE

This impressive complex was begun in 1204 on the orders of King John, on the best defensive site in Dublin. It is possible that there was a Gaelic rath here; the Vikings in their turn probably built a type of fort above the black pool where their ships lay at anchor; when Strongbow and the Anglo-Normans arrived in 1170 they built a motte and bailey here, a forerunner of the castle. Forming an impregnable 'keep' within the bounds of medieval Dublin, the castle was locked into the south-eastern corner of the city wall.

Down the years the four main towers were used for various purposes — storage, residential accommodation and even a parliament of the Pale. Henry III ordered the Great Hall to be built, specifying the dimensions as 120 feet long and 80 feet wide. The many buildings within the complex included an exchange, a chapel and a prison. In the early Tudor period the castle seems to have become run-down (perhaps reflecting the state of English rule in Ireland) because in the sixteenth century Sir Henry Sidney, one of Queen Elizabeth's Lord Deputies, undertook numerous improvements. Finally much of it burnt down in the 1680s, after which the complex began to assume its present form.

This former seat and symbol of British power in Ireland now functions as government offices. Although the castle was threatened and besieged on a number of occasions it was never taken by storm. Indeed the two escapes *from* the castle by the captured Ulster chieftain Red Hugh O'Donnell in 1591-92 were two of the more successful attempts to counter the power which it embodied. When the time came in 1922 for the representative of the British government to give possession to the Irish provisional government, it happened that his surname, Fitzalan, was as Norman as any of those who had supervised the building of the castle in 1204. The splendid state apartments, built for the viceregal court, now host national and international meetings. Some recent rebuilding has allowed archaeologists to excavate parts of the medieval walls. Amongst other finds this work has produced the exact position of the castle gate, with its twin towers and barbican.

Whatever the Anglo-Normans may have *wanted* to achieve as their influence spread out from Dublin, they failed to colonise more than the English Pale and the walled towns; this remained so up to the Tudor period.

With the English Reformation the struggle for control of Ireland acquired the crucial dimension of religious division which is still with us today.

The plantation of Ulster with English and Scottish settlers should have resulted in an ever-extending 'racial and religious purity' worthy of twentieth-century fascism. But in reality many of the Gaelic Irish lived on as tenants. The mid-seventeenth-century excesses of Oliver Cromwell established the Protestant Ascendancy which was used to rule Ireland for two and a half centuries.

By the end of the eighteenth century this Ascendancy was centred on a relatively large number of public buildings through which it controlled trade, education and government policy.

In the charter of 1192 Dublin was permitted to have guilds (rather like a union of the self-employed) of which there were twenty-eight by 1498. They regulated the trades and crafts, and administered the training process from apprenticeship, through journeyman to master.

Apprenticeship was a long process, which corresponds to the modern polytechnic or university degree. A vestige of the system survives in one of Trinity College's master of arts degrees, which is automatically awarded to successful Bachelor of Arts graduates three years after they qualify, since seven years had to pass in a trade before a man could claim the title 'master'.

Left — Trinity College Dublin **1780**, looking northwards. At this time the college was being largely rebuilt or extended to achieve the 'grand design' present today. The buildings which intersect at the centre of this picture have all disappeared, including the old green-roofed Campanile, demolished for reasons of safety.

Right — Tailors' Hall *circa* 1790, **at the time** when the United Irishmen, including Wolfe Tone, used it for meetings.

TRINITY COLLEGE

Trinity College Dublin was founded by Queen Elizabeth I, and built on the site of All Hallows, a priory dating from 1538. The college opened for the first time on 9 January 1594.

At the time of this picture the university had much in common with other such institutions in Britain. The students and faculty were all male, and almost all Protestants, indeed the (Anglican) Church of Ireland as the Established Church would have drawn on graduates for the majority of its clergy. Greek and Latin were the basis of education, but the university set up the first chair of German in Britain and Ireland. It was also progressive enough to admit Catholics at an early date, possibly as an attempt to win converts among those of the native population who could afford to attend.

Scholars (students of exceptional ability) and Fellows of the College were in effect 'company proprietors' and as today enjoyed certain privileges. A class system operated and was demonstrated by the wearing of different types of gown; those of the nobility were trimmed with gold or silver, according to rank. Some famous names from this period are Edmund Burke, Thomas Moore and Oliver Goldsmith (who left college in disgrace). Ordinary students had few responsibilities and some were wild young men who enjoyed fights in the streets with the locals, reportedly using the heavy keys to their rooms as weapons. Occasionally the town and gown conflict reached the scale of riot.

In the nineteenth century the college — like the rest of Dublin — suffered something of a social decline following the Act of Union, although new buildings continued to appear. The most prominent are the Campanile, designed by Charles Lanyon in 1852 as a substitute for the five-storey bell tower; the Graduates Memorial Building, a massive pile in the Elizabethan style; and the Museum Building of 1854, in the Venetian style.

Since the late 1960s, Trinity has more than doubled the number of full-time undergraduates and become more involved in Irish life than was possible when it was seen as the educational equivalent of Dublin Castle.

In the city beyond (see picture page 22) there is much building speculation, especially on the other side of the river. Sackville (later O'Connell)

Street has not yet formed the north/south axis which will connect with the later Westmoreland and D'Olier Streets. In the absence of any bridge at this point, ships tie up along the quay as far as Essex Bridge and the Old Custom House. On the far left stands Parliament House, glimpsed some twenty years before the Act of Union dissolved the assembly and the building was sold to the Bank of Ireland.

TAILORS' HALL

Tailors' Hall is a Queen Anne building of *circa* 1706 which was owned and used by the guild of tailors, but they also let it out to other organisations until new municipal legislation forced the guild to sell their property and turn the hall into a school.

It has been suggested that the façade was originally arranged with a main door in the centre of the present basement. This conversion may have been carried out because street levels had risen so much in this, one of the oldest and longest-inhabited parts of Dublin. The hall was approached through an imposing pedimented gateway (present today) surrounded by the shops and houses of Back Lane. Nearby stood the tower forming part of the parish church of St Michael and All Angels (see picture page 23). When the parish was dissolved in the nineteenth century this tower was incorporated into the Synod Hall, a council chamber and offices built in the 1870s and linked by a 'Bridge of Sighs' to Christ Church Cathedral. (A parish such as St Michael's was one of many parishes in a comparatively small area. Most of these sites still exist.) Beyond the tower Christ Church Cathedral stood surrounded by decaying buildings, amongst them the ruins of the old Four Courts of 1659.

With the opening of Lower Sackville (now O'Connell) Street in 1784 and the subsequent crossing of the river by the former Carlisle Bridge (where O'Connell Bridge stands today), the focus of the city's trade and social life had moved to the north and east, leaving the old city cut off from shipping and the fashionable new quarters.

Tailors' Hall has been fully restored in recent years and stands today as a reminder of much that has been lost. The surrounding area is to be redeveloped.

Royal Hospital Kilmainham Chapel interior 1849. The chapel ceiling was a breathtaking array of what could be called continuous still life, with everything from plasterwork carrot to winged heads! The present ceiling (1902) is an exact *papier-mâché* replica of the original.

Royal Hospital Kilmainham exterior 1780, looking southwards. In this picture the Royal Hospital is already a century old. From left to right behind the northern façade are the chapel, entrance hall, dining hall and Master's lodgings.

ROYAL HOSPITAL KILMAINHAM

Founded by the Duke of Ormonde, this institution was built in the vicinity of a medieval priory, part of whose ruins may have been used to provide the stone tracing of the large chapel window (see picture page 26).

The Royal Hospital Kilmainham is so called

The old book-plate of the Royal Hospital Library shows the harp of Ireland subjected to the English Crown. The surrounding militaria include various flags and a trumpet. Further down are pikes, three drums and a set of armour.

because it provided living accommodation for army pensioners maintained at the government's expense. There was also an infirmary for the sick, built in 1711. The Royal Hospital building looks forward to Dublin's greatest architecture in the eighteenth century; here was building of a style and scale previously unknown in Ireland. The overall impression is French because the design is based on Les Invalides in Paris. Construction began in 1680 and the first residents were there by 1684.

Living accommodation was provided for three hundred army veterans, with spacious lodgings for the Master. After a life of campaigning, these old soldiers must have appreciated the peace and beauty of such surroundings, with grounds to the west and a formal garden on the northern side. If the weather was bad, the men could take their exercise in the shelter of the cloister-like quadrangle. Everyday life would perhaps have been a gentle reminder of army routine.

In 1687 there were very few church buildings in which Catholics could worship. Many of the Kilmainham pensioners must have been Catholics and it is recorded that the authorities did at some time arrange for Mass to be said, in spite of the severe Penal Laws which outlawed the saying of Mass.

After Irish independence in 1922 veterans lived in the Royal Hospital until 1927, when those remaining were offered places in the similar Chelsea Hospital in London. Meanwhile the building was used and maintained by government departments. After a thorough restoration in the mid-1980s, the Royal Hospital Kilmainham opened in 1986 as a national centre for the arts, including display space for the National Museum, and conference facilities.

The western gate at the Royal Hospital Kilmainham is a striking Gothic Revival structure built in 1812 to a design by Francis Johnston. The gate originally stood on a quay at the bottom of Watling Street but was removed because of traffic congestion after Kingsbridge (now Heuston) Railway Station was built. On the left just inside the gate are two cemeteries, in one of which Robert Emmet who led the uprising of 1803 was buried. By contrast the other cemetery contains the graves of Royal Hospital pensioners and of British troops killed in the 1916 Rising.

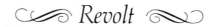

Revolt

In the eighteenth century the damage to the Irish economy which could be inflicted at will by London was one of the grievances which affected Protestant and Catholic merchants alike. Ulster Presbyterians were penalised for not being Church of Ireland (Anglican) and at times made common cause with the native population — although Ulster Protestants today are often surprised by the discovery of a radical, anti-English ancestry.

Protestants led groups such as the United Irishmen whose aim was to set up an independent Republic of Ireland along French lines. In 1798 the government moved against them, resulting in the deaths of leaders such as Lord Edward Fitzgerald and Wolfe Tone. London, alarmed by the danger to itself of French influence in Ireland, prepared the way for the Act of Union (passed in 1800, enacted 1801), which dampened hopes of independence for three-quarters of a century.

Kilmainham Jail interior 1900.
This impressive central space
had three floors any one of
which could be contained and
isolated through the grille
system.

KILMAINHAM JAIL

Kilmainham Jail is built on a ridge over the river Camac. Completed in 1796 it was normally used to house prisoners of Dublin county. But it often served the British government as a high-security detention centre for nationalist activists. Among these was the United Irishman Thomas Addis Emmet, held in 1798. Five years later his brother Robert was taken from the jail to his execution in front of St Catherine's Church, Thomas Street, after organising an abortive *coup d'état*.

Living conditions for prisoners could vary greatly according to social rank; it is known that wives were even allowed as a privilege to be left alone with their husbands. Charles Stewart Parnell spent time in this jail. Although a Protestant of the landlord class, Parnell became chairman of the Irish parliamentarians in the Westminster elections of 1880. As a result of Gladstone's Land Act of the following year (which began to break the mould of the landlord system) Parnell was able to press for Home Rule, using language which resulted in his imprisonment. Parnell's release was secured in 1882 under the terms of his 'Kilmainham Treaty' negotiated with Gladstone. His anti-English stance was not new in the family, since his mother was descended from radical Northern Irish Protestants who had emigrated to North America before the War of Independence, where they had fought against the British in 1776 and 1812.

Kilmainham Jail was filled with the activists of Easter Week 1916 and it was here that Padraic Pearse and James Connolly, amongst others, were executed. This action of the British government was decisive in turning Irish public opinion in favour of the insurgents.

Kilmainham Jail had fallen into ruins by the 1950s, but was later restored as a museum, opened by President de Valera (himself a former detainee). It is not an attractive building and would doubtless have been demolished had it not come to serve as a memorial of the struggle for independence. In 1986 the government took over the museum from the voluntary committee who had restored it.

When a city reaches a certain 'critical mass' it has enough power of attraction to draw forth from its hinterland — or further afield — labour and talents which make it a unique environment. The city fosters these energies and accomplishments in close proximity one to another, offering opportunities of encounter which do not exist in a rural society. This interaction is only to be expected in cities which have grown up on continental trade routes, or in a city such as London which has for centuries been the largest in Europe.

That Dublin as the capital of an island should have developed into a sophisticated urban centre in the course of a century is against all expectations. Whereas a hundred years previously Dublin was in the grip of Oliver Cromwell and the English Civil War, in the 1740s this was the city where elegant ladies and gentlemen left houses decorated with rococo plasterwork to attend the first performance of Handel's _Messiah_.

Musicians and singers from all over Europe were attracted to Dublin. The arts flourished, and catalogues of private art collections show that aristocratic Dubliners possessed some very fine paintings, as well as having fitting houses in which to hang them. Another important indicator is that commercial draughtsmen and freelance artists came to work in the city, amongst them the aquatint artist James Malton and the map-maker John Rocque.

The basis of much of this prosperity was doubtless the existence of an Irish parliament.

St Stephen's Green West. These three street elevations show the same stretch of the Green in three different years: 1750 (top), 1810 and 1830.

ST STEPHEN'S GREEN WEST

In the eighteenth century, as today, Dublin had certain areas where one social class predominated. But the city as a whole was quite compact, and there could be a social mix of grandees living on the main street and traders living in the lanes at their backs. St Stephen's Green, as befitted its long history as a common, was developed as a residential area by gentlemen and traders alike.

The Green had been enclosed by the Corporation in the mid-seventeenth century and was then divided up into building lots. The scheme was not a speculative development since the ground rents were to provide an income for the King's Hospital School (an institution which survives today, although not on its original site). The idea of St Stephen's Green as a city square therefore predates any of the great developments which turned the north side of the city, centred on Gardiner's Mall (now O'Connell Street), into the most important residential quarter for much of the eighteenth century. However, the decision in 1744 to build Leinster House south of the river is held to have begun the decline of the north side and no doubt enhanced the social desirability of St Stephen's Green.

The picture on page 33 shows the same stretch of St Stephen's Green in three different years.

Top, 1750. In the eighteenth century this side of the square, called 'French Walk', was characterised by many residents of Huguenot origin, with names such as Charles de la Bouchetiers and Solomon Barbault. Huguenots were French Protestants and mostly middle class. They had been more or less tolerated by the French government until the revocation of the Edict of Nantes in 1685. There followed an exodus of these hard-working and industrious people, causing a 'brain drain' to Protestant-ruled countries such as Prussia, Great Britain and Ireland, which greatly benefited from their arrival. The 'Dutch Billy' house, many of which were built in Dublin, dates from this period and is obviously Continental in origin, also known as 'Franco-Dutch'.

On the extreme left is where York Street

intersects. Behind the wall was a Quaker burial ground until 1805. The carriage is typical of the period, as are the two sedan-chair-men carrying a distinguished passenger. Sedan chairs were the mark of large towns and cities, just as fleets of taxis are today. They would have carried their passengers short distances within the city, perhaps between appointments and social engagements. The alleyway, right of centre, was originally called 'Rapparee Alley' (perhaps indicating a place of 'low resort'), now known as Glover's Alley.

Middle, 1810. The Surgeons' Hall (left) was built in 1809 on the site of the burial ground (see above), whilst the two houses next to it were demolished. In 1778 Robert Emmet was born in the house to the right of Glover's Alley. His father was a physician by profession. The horses pulling the dray (centre) could have belonged to one of three major breweries: Thwaites, Andrews or Guinness (whose business was over fifty years old in that year).

Bottom, 1830. In 1827 the Surgeons' Hall was extended by the now Royal College of Surgeons to take in the whole length between York Street and Glover's Alley. By this time the majority of householders along French Walk are recorded as being traders or professional men; however the Huguenot presence continued at least until 1841, when a Mr Charles le Bas was still living in No. 132.

The College of Surgeons was the scene of a gun-battle between British troops and Irish insurgents under Countess Markievicz in the Easter Rising of 1916. In recent years St Stephen's Green has seen much redevelopment, especially along this western side. The three houses next to Surgeons' were demolished to make way for the new commercial centre at the top of Grafton Street.

Up until the 1960s, the St Stephen's Green area must have acted like an educational magnet each day, as schoolchildren, students and scholars arrived to study in the educational institutions which formed part of it — four major secondary schools (none of which survives in the area), the National Library, the National Museum and University College.

PARLIAMENT HOUSE

Sir Edward Lovett Pearce designed the Parliament House in 1729. A year later he took over from Colonel Thomas Burgh as Surveyor General of Ireland. Considering the severity of Burgh's design for the Library of Trinity College (which resembles his barracks, now called Collins Barracks) it is fortunate that Pearce was given the commission and not Burgh, as it allowed him to build his finest work.

Parliament House is shown here surrounded by houses, shops and taverns, many of them built in the 'Dutch Billy' style common between 1680 and 1730. The famous equestrian statue of King William III standing in College Green (left) was such a target for insult that a guardhouse was placed next to it in the eighteenth century. It was finally blown up in 1929.

The picture shows an official opening of parliament, with the townsfolk looking on as the elite emerge from the building. Parliament was far from representing the people who would have stopped to observe such a scene, since only a few of them were allowed to vote and the anti-Catholic Penal Laws were still in force. Members of Trinity College used to be allowed to enter the Visitors' Gallery, but students were subsequently excluded because of their bad behaviour.

In 1792 the great dome of the House of Commons (centre) accidentally caught fire and was never properly restored. James Gandon designed a portico for the House of Lords which was added in the 1780s. Up to the Act of Union in 1801, Parliament House comprised two chambers, the Commons and the Lords on the British model.

The Irish parliament, like the members of the university, were almost exclusively Protestants. When the British government intervened to protect its own economy at the expense of Ireland's trade, this tended to foster a nationalist sense amongst the Irish Protestants, for whom the threat of a Catholic terror seems to have receded since the Battle of the Boyne (1690). But Irish Protestants who dreamt of an independent state must have had grave doubts about the future of their own class, for example after the installation of a French-style republic, which seems to be what Wolfe Tone intended in 1796

Parliament House 1760. An impressive and serene building, Parliament House was begun in 1729 to a design by Edward Lovett Pearce.

and 1798. Parliamentarians who wished to bring about greater self-determination for Ireland included Henry Grattan, who is shown addressing the chamber in Francis Wheatley's famous picture of the Irish House of Commons. In the eighteen-year period up to 1800, this parliament could imagine that it was free to pass laws without reference to London, but in reality its independence could be overridden by the British government, as finally happened in 1800, when important figures in the Irish Parliament were given incentives (the Union peerages) to assent to the Act of Union.

When the Act came into force on 1 January 1801, direct rule from Westminster abolished the need for a parliament house in Dublin, and the two chambers were to be removed. The House of Commons was dismantled but the House of Lords survives almost intact with certain furnishings which the Board of the Bank of Ireland have restored to their original home. This includes the silver-gilt Speaker's mace of *circa* 1766. The exterior of the building was thoroughly cleaned and restored in the 1970s.

KING'S INNS AND HENRIETTA STREET

Henrietta Street branches off from Bolton Street and rises up a hill to reach the King's Inns. The houses are exceptionally grand and belong to the earliest of the great building ventures of Luke Gardiner, who also laid out the fashionable Mall that survives as the upper part of O'Connell Street. The hill on which Henrietta Street stands was originally called 'Primate's Hill' because the Archbishop of Armagh had a house there, on the site now occupied by the Library (1827), bottom left in the picture (page 40).

The houses were designed by a number of different architects, presumably the best available, since the Gardiners themselves lived in No. 10, the cream-painted one in this picture. The interiors of these houses are in the finest tradition of Georgian design, however some have been neglected or even sold off when the houses were divided up to become tenements, as early as the first decade of this century. Happily the interior of No. 10 has been well maintained by a convent.

The building which closes the street is the King's Inns, designed by James Gandon and his partner Henry Baker, with later additions by Francis Johnston. Although the foundation stone was laid in 1795, full construction did not begin until 1802, and the building was completed by 1817. Later in the century two minor wings were added to the façade as seen from Constitution Hill.

The Inns are used by 'benchers' (senior barristers and judges) for dinners during the law terms. Also lectures for diploma and degree courses are given, and the library is used by both students and barristers.

Beyond the King's Inns on the left is the Royal Canal Harbour, reached by way of the Foster Aqueduct. This token of the coming industrial age itself gave way to new technology when the harbour was filled in in 1877 to become the forecourt of the Broadstone Station, which was closed in the 1930s. Henrietta Street remained a prestigious address well into the nineteenth century. The street probably owes its survival to being closed to vehicular traffic at one end, in addition to its comparative remoteness.

FITZWILLIAM SQUARE

Fitzwilliam and Merrion Squares were particularly fine urban spaces for the richer inhabitants of Dublin. The very richest, especially aristocrats, would have lived in magnificent stone mansions.

Many householders in this area would also have owned a country residence, living on the rent from estate property. Others would have been 'first class' civil servants and members of the professions. Although most residents would have been Protestant, there were also upper-class Catholics, educated perhaps in England, whose sentiments could have been nationalist. The lifestyle here would not have differed so very much from that of similar people in London or Edinburgh.

The house layout was typically: basement with servants' work area; hall level with a study and dining-room; first floor with double drawing-room; second floor, three or four bedrooms; top floors, small rooms and the nursery. This last seems to have been kept as far away as possible from adult ears. 'Nurse' spent longer with the

The King's Inns and Henrietta
Street *circa* 1830. The Inns are
still **run by** the legal profession,
but many of the fine private
houses on Henrietta Street have
long been neglected.

40

Fitzwilliam Square *circa* 1840. An unusual bird's eye view of one of Dublin's smaller squares. Fitzwilliam Street runs north/south on the righthand side of this picture. Fitzwilliam Square was not completed until well into the nineteenth century.

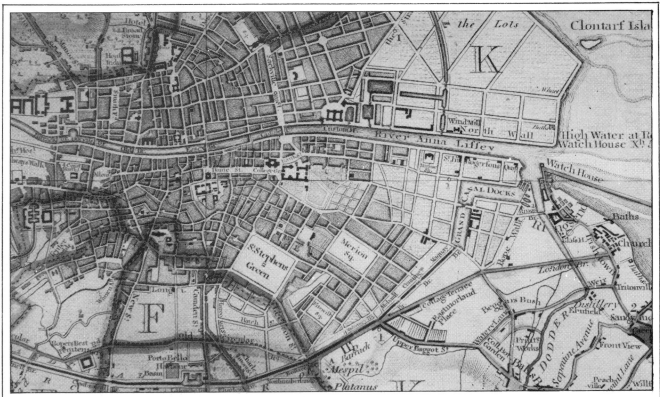

Part of John **Taylor's map** of Dublin (1828). Georgian Dublin is concentrated both north and south of the river in the **central part** of this plan. Fitzwilliam Square, south of Merrion Square, is still incomplete.

children than a socially active mother did. In addition to the 'army of servants' needed to run such houses, there might also have been a gardener and a coachman. If a family could not afford a coach they would have needed a pony and trap at the very least. The streets were cobbled in areas which saw a lot of traffic. Cobbles were laid in certain patterns which helped to reduce wear, especially at busy junctions.

As a change from indoors, residents of Fitzwilliam Square had the right to use the grounds of the Square, and children were taken there by the nurse.

'At-homes' were given by ladies on a particular day, perhaps on a regular basis. Tea was served at these gatherings which were meant to be casual. Dances — often for well over a hundred guests — were held in winter, and at such times these squares must have had the air of a large club.

Today Fitzwilliam Square survives in good condition; even the man-hole covers are of interest. Its present use is as a mixture of offices and living space; the presence of medical and legal practices is a reminder of earlier days.

THE ROTUNDA

This picture shows Dublin almost at its peak. In the foreground is the Rotunda Hospital, the first purpose-built maternity hospital in the world. It was built to a design by the German architect Richard Cassels at the instigation of Dr Bartholomew Mosse. The Rotunda was and still is a great institution. Its pleasure gardens were the focus of this elegant quarter of Dublin, which could compare favourably with London (Vauxhall Gardens) and Bath in having such amenities. But Dublin was special because the Rotunda allowed the leaders of society to combine entertainment with charity, since the former financed the latter.

In the gardens may be seen some of the entertainments available to those who had subscribed to the hospital's charity schemes and events: a large bowling green, an orchestra (meaning a venue suitable for music recitals), walks and shrubberies, and a coffee tent, the whole illuminated for soirées.

The square surrounding the gardens was near the northernmost extent of the city, with fields just beyond the next street. The houses were built for the rich by property speculators, chief amongst them Luke Gardiner. The finest house — almost like an Italian palazzo — is in the centre of the terrace opposite: this belonged to Lord Charlemont, who also owned the Casino at Marino. Charlemont House is now the Municipal Gallery of Modern Art. The carriages seen here would have belonged to such people. Sedan chairs were the most common public transport, and in the top right-hand corner of this square there stood a shelter for the men who plied this trade. The shelter was demolished in 1943.

Almost no expense was spared in the building of the Rotunda. It has a fine baroque chapel with a ceiling unlike any other in Ireland. At one time the tower was topped with a gilded cradle, crown and ball which cost £137. As the years passed, the Round Room (the circular brick building) was built as part of a 'pleasure complex' which included a card-room, tea-room and ballroom.

A similar view today would show how much the hospital has expanded into the former pleasure gardens. Most of the houses have survived as offices, whilst the buildings intended for public entertainment still perform this function. These include the Ambassador Cinema (inside the actual 'rotunda' — the assembly hall of 1764) and the Gate Theatre, within another function room dating from 1784. The Gate occupies the space over the splendid 'Pillar Room' which has recently been restored as a research centre within the Rotunda Trust.

The Gate Theatre was set up in 1929 and greatly improved the quality of drama and its presentation in Ireland. Two of its directors, Hilton Edwards and Micheál macLiammóir, spent most of their working lives there, presenting new plays and some other works which might not otherwise have been performed in Dublin. The new theatre managed to survive financially through the efforts of the then Lord and Lady Longford, whose vision seems to have matched that of the original subscribers to the Rotunda Lying-in Hospital and pleasure gardens.

The Rotunda Hospital and Gardens 1776, surrounded by Rutland (now Parnell) Square. A composition such as this shows why Dublin was described as second only to London in urban sophistication.

The Penal Laws began to be enacted in Ireland at the end of the seventeenth century. Their aim was a Protestant Ireland wrested from the power of the Catholic Church, and they were most successful in dispossessing the Gaelic population. If these laws failed to convert the minds of Ireland's Catholics, they at least utterly degraded their material circumstances. Whereas French minority Protestants had either been murdered or expelled from their own country, the Irish Catholics were to live on in abject poverty, without the right to property, education or representation in parliament.

In the eighteenth century many Protestants recognised how unjust the Penal Laws were. Under influence from London, Catholics in 1793 gained the right to vote in elections, but the aristocratic Irish parliament could not risk further changes without endangering their very existence. In fact this did occur with the passing of the Act of Union (1800) which brought about direct rule from London, and it took almost thirty years before Daniel O'Connell's mass movement for liberation brought the effects of the Penal Laws to the fore once again. Within one year of his election to Westminster the Catholic Emancipation Act was passed. It may have removed the conditions under which the degradation of Catholics had come about, but it could restore only the minimum of what they had lost. Indeed with the potato Famine only fifteen years away, they had still more to lose.

Church of St John the Baptist, Thomas Street (1860). Present day. Industrialisation in the last century seems to have led to confusion in certain areas of culture. Architecture suffered from great confusion, verging on crisis. The century which began with the simplicity (and sometimes severity) of Neo-Classical architecture ended with a riot of different styles — Gothic, Byzantine-Venetian and Florentine Renaissance, amongst others. The crisis is illustrated here by St John's Church in Thomas Street. It was designed by Augustus Pugin, a zealous convert to Catholicism, who looked back to the fourteenth century for his inspiration. This taste was not endorsed by Cardinal Newman (founder of the Catholic University) who preferred the Classical styles.

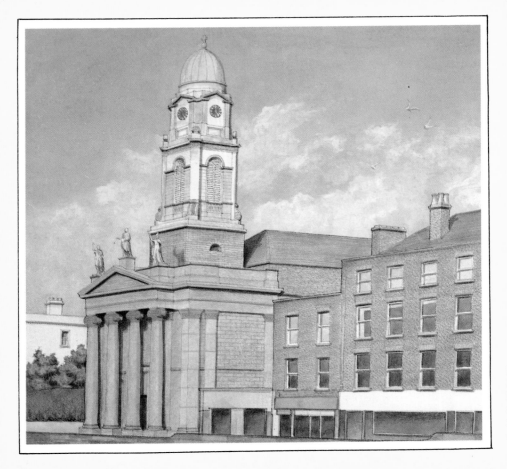

St Paul's Church, Arran Quay. For many years Dublin's quays have suffered from neglect, but along some stretches the river reflects buildings of quality such as St Paul's and the Four Courts.

ST PAUL'S CHURCH, ARRAN QUAY

The Catholic Emancipation Act of 1829 allowed Catholics complete freedom to practise their faith. Since the Established (Anglican) Church still possessed most of the ancient church sites there was a sustained building effort by the Catholic Church in the 1830s and 1840s. Many Dublin churches of this period are substantial buildings in the Greek or Italian styles. However some of them suffer from their location, and in one case this was because the Church feared to occupy too prominent a position on Sackville Street. As a result the Pro-Cathedral is out of scale with Marlborough Street and would need more free space in front of it; the main body of the Franciscan church on Merchants' Quay seems to fear comparison with the Four Courts and stands behind the buildings which line the quay.

However at least two of the Catholic churches of this period gain from their siting. St Audoen's rises next to the Church of Ireland church of the same name, on ground above the Franciscan church. It was built thus on the same ridge as Christ Church Cathedral and the church of St Michael and All Angels (whose tower forms part of the former Synod Hall) on roughly the same level as Dublin Castle. All this reinforces what has been said about St Audoen's, that it looks 'like an impregnable fortress'; indeed part of the medieval city wall lies just below to the east.

The other well-sited church is St Paul's, Arran Quay (see picture, page 48), a fine addition to this stretch of the river Liffey. Built on the attractive curve of the river, the church does not in any way confront the Four Courts, which are nearby, but acts rather as an 'attendant beauty'.

All these Catholic churches, except the Pro-Cathedral, are by the architect Patrick Byrne, who was able to build in a style which blended with Dublin's eighteenth-century architecture.

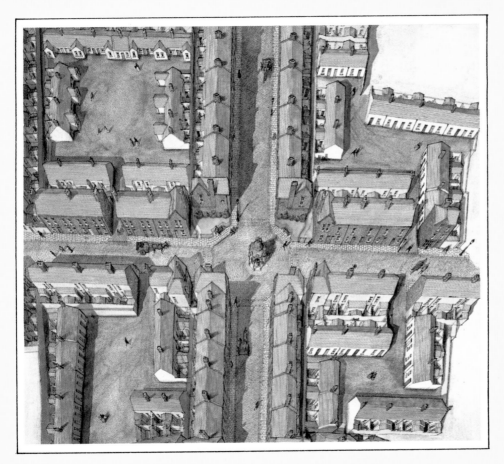

Gray Street 1900. A bird's-eye view of an area of the Liberties redeveloped in the nineteenth century. Compare this with upper class housing in Fitzwilliam Square, page 41.

In the nineteenth century the north-east of Ireland began to build up a manufacturing base of the kind found in Scotland and the north of England. By contrast, inner Dublin declined during this period and ended the century with some of the worst slums in northern Europe. However the Victorian suburbs added greatly to the overall size of Dublin, especially the middle-class area on the south side which extended in an almost unbroken swathe out along the bay to Kingstown (now Dun Laoghaire) and beyond.

Transport improved greatly in the early part of the century with the arrival of the Grand and Royal Canals. The Dublin and Kingstown Railway opened in 1834 and in later years other lines connected Dublin to the country, with fine terminal buildings at Kingsbridge (1848) (now Heuston) Station and Broadstone (1850).

Breweries and distilleries seem to have been the main growth industries in nineteenth-century Dublin. These family concerns were major employers and in the case of Guinness's did much to improve workers' living standards. Not far from the St James's Gate Guinness Brewery were Roe's Distillery (now part of Guinness), Power's Distillery (now the National College of Art and Design) and D'Arcy's Brewery. Across the river was Jameson's Bow Street Distillery.

ARTISANS' DWELLINGS IN THE LIBERTIES

Economic stagnation after the Act of Union in 1801 (which took away the Irish parliament) and the Famine of the 1840s had made parts of Dublin into slum areas of overcrowded tenements. Hardest hit were casual labourers who needed to live as near as possible to their potential workplace. Artisans were slightly better off — they were skilled workers who had served an apprenticeship. Trade associations could give these people protection against sickness and unemployment. However the market changed considerably during the nineteenth century, so that trades such as tanning and tailoring declined, whilst printing and brewing were growth industries.

In the middle of the century almost half of the population lived in one-room tenement accommodation. This situation was partly relieved by the work of Dublin Corporation and various organisations such as the Dublin Artisans Dwelling Company, who built the houses shown here (page 50), completed in 1884.

Clockwise from the top right, the squares are Gray Square, Reginald Square, Meath Square and Brabazon Square. This building layout seems to look forward to the more sensitive Dublin Corporation housing developments in the inner city beginning in the 1970s, after the full horror of high-rise flats for lower income groups became recognised.

The street at the base of this picture is the Coombe, one of the oldest areas in Dublin, and in the nineteenth century a centre of squalid over-crowding. (At the turn of the century Dublin had the highest death rate in the United Kingdom.) It was expensive to demolish the tenements and compensate the owners. Furthermore the cottages built as replacements were no great blessing for the poorest citizens, who could still not afford the rent. These three- and four-roomed dwellings with no bathroom were often home to very large families of perhaps fourteen children, by comparison the 'better-off'!

In the centre of this picture is a drinking fountain in an exuberant oriental style. Unfortunately it was almost completely destroyed in a traffic accident. An almost identical structure, the Victoria Memorial in Dun Laoghaire, was blown up in 1981.

Dublin owes its survival in the twentieth century to that very distance from the Continent which makes the sophistication of the eighteenth century city so remarkable. Although much of O'Connell Street was destroyed in the Easter Rising and the Civil War (which claimed also the interiors of the Four Courts and the Custom House), Dublin had suffered little building damage when compared with what Europe lost in the Second World War. After post-war recovery, living standards in western Europe rose to new levels and Ireland experienced a share of this: many young Dubliners now aspire to a lifestyle not unlike that of their European and North American contemporaries; the shopping streets of Dublin are bright, shining examples of how a by no means rich country can support a convincing 'consumer society', at least within the bounds of the capital city.

But in architectural terms there may be too high a price to pay where the historical core of a city falls victim to economic success. In Dublin it is plain that economic pressures to build high-rise office blocks have been greatest in areas where they cause most damage. Whilst on the one hand no major public building has been demolished in this century, it is the Georgian housing stock which has borne the brunt of wholesale destruction in many instances. Interiors have been ruined or sold off, and it is just this kind of irretrievable loss which was suffered by many Continental cities in the course of a full-scale war.

In 1987 the Custom House Development Authority held an international competition which asked architects and developers to plan the revitalisation of the dock to the east of the Custom House, James Gandon's masterpiece. The winning scheme seems to indicate that some important lessons have been learnt about how best to approach the redevelopment of Dublin city centre. Rather than making aggressive gestures at the surrounding architecture, the designs are for a low-rise complex which will form a vibrant new quarter on ground that would otherwise be redundant.

O'CONNELL STREET

Originally called Sackville Street, this major concourse grew out of a number of schemes beginning in the mid-eighteenth century. At that time Luke Gardiner laid out the Mall which stretched from roughly halfway along the present street up to the Rotunda Hospital. This combined with the Rotunda pleasure gardens to make a fashionable quarter whose aristocratic scale would have contrasted greatly with the streets of the medieval city.

Later in the same century the street was extended as far as the river Liffey, where the Carlisle Bridge (1790) carried it across to the other side. The bridging of the river at this new point was feasible only after Gandon's Custom House was built downstream of it. On the south bank a range of buildings gave the appearance of stage-set flats, an idea reinforced by the backdrop of Westmoreland and D'Olier Streets.

The picture (page 55) shows O'Connell Street just after the end of 'the Emergency', as the Second World War was called in Ireland. Much of the street has been rebuilt after the destruction of 1916 and 1922, so that there survive only a few of the original Georgian townhouses such as those that line Merrion Square. The appearance of O'Connell Street has in many ways reflected the politics of the day. The Nelson Pillar, completed in 1810, was the centrepiece of this major thoroughfare. Erected in the decade following the Act of Union with Great Britain, the Pillar was a potent symbol of British presence. The General Post Office (left of the Pillar) was completed in 1818, some two years after work had begun on the Pro-Cathedral, in the relative obscurity of

O'Connell Street 1945. Today this thoroughfare is often filled with cars, buses and lorries. O'Connell Street has seen a lot of twentieth-century Irish history and was severely damaged both in the 1916 Rising and the Civil War (1922).

Marlborough Street. Only with the O'Connell Monument of 1879-83 would Sackville Street acquire an Irish figurehead to compete with the tokens of British influence.

During the Easter Rising of 1916 a republic was proclaimed at the General Post Office (GPO). The building was later shelled and burnt out, and has since become a monument in itself whilst still performing its original function. Other buildings in the street were not restored to their original character, and this part of Dublin is 'international' in the worst sense of the word. One building which is remembered with great affection by many Dubliners is the Metropole cinema and ballroom (left of the GPO), now replaced by a chain store.

As a point in their favour, the planners who controlled the rebuilding of O'Connell Street in the 1920s seem to have had strictly enforced rules about heights of buildings, so that dull or mundane architecture was at least prevented from grabbing too much attention.

In 1966, the fiftieth anniversary of the Rising, Nelson Pillar was blown up and the stump later demolished. Few people would have objected to the removal of the statue of Nelson, but many Dubliners still regret the loss of this famous landmark, which was also the hub of the tram network, discontinued 1948-49. The Pillar provided spectacular views of the city from the railing 108 feet above O'Connell Street.

1 The Parnell Monument, 60 feet tall, was designed by Augustus St Gaudens, an American sculptor of Irish origin. It was erected in 1911 and bears a quotation from Charles Stewart Parnell's speeches about Irish nationhood. His statue and the quotation are surmounted by an uncrowned harp symbolising Irish independence.

2 The Nelson Pillar, 134 feet tall, was built in 1808-9 with funds raised by a committee of bankers and merchants thankful for Nelson's victory over Napoleon at Trafalgar. It was designed by William Wilkins at Norwich, with Francis Johnston as consultant architect. The sturdy neo-Classicism of the pillar was later complimented by Johnston's General Post Office nearby. The pillar was blown up in 1966.

3 The O'Connell Monument, 40 feet tall, by John Henry Foley, won a competition for the design of a fitting tribute to the architect of Catholic Emancipation. Foley did not live to finish the work, and Thomas Brock designed the allegorical figures which surround the base. The monument was completed in 1882. It stands in the street just before the bridge, both renamed in O'Connell's honour.

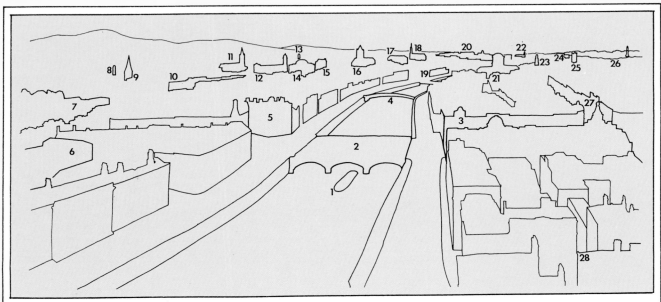

Dublin and the River Liffey 1950

1 Guinness barge
2 O'Connell Bridge
3 O'Connell Street
4 Ha'penny Bridge
5 Ballast Office (replicated 1979)
6 Theatre Royal (demolished 1962)
7 Trinity College Dublin
8 Mercer's Hospital
9 St Andrew Street
10 Dame Street

11 St Patrick's Cathedral
12 Dublin Castle
13 St Nicholas of Myra Church
14 City Hall
15 Newcomen's Bank
16 Christ Church Cathedral
17 St Audoen's Catholic Church
18 St John's Church, Thomas Street
19 Wood Quay
20 Guinness Brewery and former
   windmill

21 Four Courts
22 Royal Hospital Kilmainham
23 St Paul's Church Arran Quay
24 Heuston (formerly Kingsbridge)
   Railway Station
25 St Michan's Church
26 Phoenix Park and the Wellington
   Monument
27 Abbey Street
28 Rear of Abbey Theatre

DUBLIN AND THE LIFFEY

This view shows the centre of Dublin in the late 1940s, before the boom in office building. In the austerity of the post-war years much of the traffic consisted of black-coloured cars and green buses, with a large number of bicycles. The Guinness barges were a familiar sight — here the only craft shown on the river — as they travelled between the brewery and the port of Dublin. Many citizens remember watching out for these boats with the special hinged smokestacks which had to be lowered when passing under bridges. The barges were dispensed with in 1961, but the Guinness freighters in the same livery of blue and cream are still loaded at George's Quay.

The interaction of river and city is part of the richness of any urban centre lucky enough to possess an elegant or impressive waterway passing through its heart. The Liffey rises in the Wicklow mountains some twelve miles due south of Dublin city centre. It drops quickly to meander through low terrain for most of its course, performing a 180° turn by the time it arrives in Dublin. At Islandbridge a weir marks the height to which tide and saltwater rise. From here down, the river has for centuries been crossed by an assortment of bridges and ferries, and channelled by the building of quays and the encroachment of reclaimed ground.

With the formal quays by then in place, Dubliners have had less and less contact with the river since the early nineteenth century — one of Jack B. Yeats's most famous pictures, 'The Liffey Swim' 1928, (National Gallery of Ireland), is a notable exception to this trend. It was once not unusual to see rafts bearing timber downriver to the docks, as in some of James Malton's eighteenth-century prints, where he also seems to hint at a water-taxi service redolent more of Venice than the Dublin we know today.

In this picture the old Dublin seems to hold its breath before being pushed into the years of industrial expansion and the new role as a European Community capital. This was the Dublin of Brendan Behan and Patrick Kavanagh, of Flann O'Brien as he walked between the Custom House and *The Irish Times*.

UNIVERSITY COLLEGE DUBLIN

University College Dublin has its origins in the Catholic University founded by John Henry Newman in 1854. He was an English academic who came to Dublin to found a seat of learning for Catholics, some twenty-five years after the Catholic Emancipation Act. The new institution on Stephen's Green was intended to keep Catholics out of Trinity College Dublin and the Queen's Colleges (Cork, Belfast and Galway), known as the 'godless' colleges because the Catholic Church did not control them.

Newman resigned in 1858 and the Catholic University more or less declined until 1883 — for example there were only twenty students there in 1873. However, fortunes improved after 1879, when Newman was made the English cardinal, and in 1883 University College came into existence as part of the Royal University, later the National University of Ireland.

By 1955 UCD had acquired most of the land at Belfield, the new site in the southern suburbs. The university had outgrown its city-centre accommodation and the need to move became pressing. Work began on a science building, but in 1963 architects were invited to enter an international competition to find an overall designer for the campus. This was won by Andrzej Wejchert, an architect from Poland who subsequently set up a practice in Ireland.

Belfield was designed in the modernist style. As the years pass and vast new buildings are added, University College is becoming a 'mega-structure', with everything but residential accommodation. Belfield is a showcase of efficient modernism in an excellent setting. The pool at the centre of this picture does much to enhance the site; trees and shrubs make it a pleasant environment. There are ten thousand full-time students in University College, and at lunchtime the dining hall caters for four thousand people at two sittings.

As a tribute to the most famous alumnus of University College Dublin, a bust of James Joyce has been placed near the entrance to the arts and commerce building, just above the centre of the picture (see page 62).

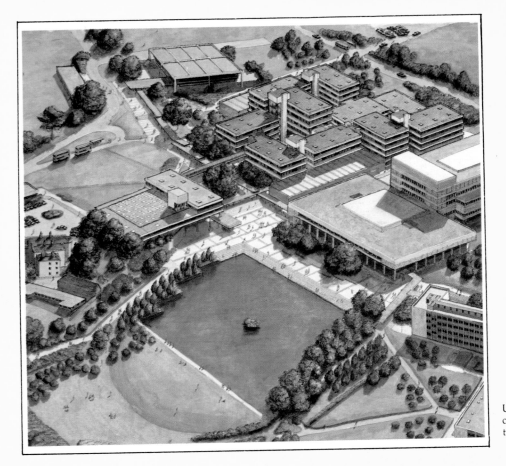

University College Dublin. A large
complex of modernist architecture in
the southern suburbs of Dublin.

CHRONOLOGY

888 King Sitric takes throne.

936 Dublin razed by Donnchad Donn.

997 Vikings mint first coins in Dublin.

1014 Battle of Clontarf: Brian Boru and allies defeat rebel King of Leinster and end the Viking expansion.

1028 King Sitric and Bishop Dunan found Christ Church Cathedral.

1093 St Michan's Church built.

1171 St Audoen's Church built

1172 Strongbow and Normans rebuild Christ Church Cathedral. Henry II gives the city 'to his men of Bristol' in the First Charter of Dublin.

1229 Position of Mayor created.

1304 Great fire destroys north side of city, including St Mary's Abbey.

1317 Edward Bruce and 20,000 men approach Dublin. A new city wall is built to guard against them.

1329 Paving of city streets begins.

1454 Irish people evicted from city. They settle at Irishtown.

1487 Ten-year-old pretender, Lambert Simnel, crowned Edward VI at Christ Church.

1534 Revolt of Silken Thomas.

1551 First book printed in Ireland — the Book of Common Prayer.

1587 Red Hugh O'Donnell, heir of The O'Donnell of Donegal, is imprisoned by the English in Dublin Castle.

1592 Queen Elizabeth founds Trinity College.

1610 First map of Dublin drawn (Speed's map).

1649 Cromwell arrives at Ringsend with 12,000 troops.

1662 Phoenix Park and St Stephen's Green laid out.

1667 Jonathan Swift, future Dean of St Patrick's and author, born.

1680 Royal Hospital Kilmainham built.

1690 King James retreats hastily via Dublin after his routing at the Battle of the Boyne.

1691 King William of Orange presents new mayoral chain of office.

1702 First public library, Marsh's, opened next to St Patrick's Cathedral.

1706 Oldest remaining guild hall, Tailors' Hall, constructed on Back Lane.

1729 Parliament buildings, now the Bank of Ireland, built on College Green.

1730 Henrietta Street developed on north side.

1742 Handel's *Messiah* performed for the first time at the Musick Hall, Fishamble Street.

1745 Leinster House (now Dáil Eireann) built.

1750 Dr Bartholomew Mosse founds the first public maternity hospital, the Rotunda.

1759 Guinness's Brewery opens at St James's Gate.

1769 The Royal Exchange (or City Hall) built on Cork Hill.

1773 King's Hospital built on Blackhall Place.

1781 Work on James Gandon's Customs House begun.

1781 Britain grants Ireland independent parliament.

1784 Sackville Street (O'Connell St.) and area laid out.

1785 Work on Gandon's Four Courts begins.

1788 Kilmainham Jail built on the river Camac.

1791 Fitzwilliam Square and Mountjoy Square laid out. Power's and Jameson's distilleries open. The United Irishmen meet for the first time.

1795 Gandon designs King's Inns.

1800 Act of Union abolishes Irish parliament.

1803 Robert Emmet executed for murder of Lord Kilwarden. Parliament House converted to Bank of Ireland.

1804 Construction begins on 21 Martello Towers, to be used as defences against Napoleon.

1806 Royal College of Surgeons erected on St Stephen's Green.

1808 Nelson Pillar erected on Sackville Street.

1814 Construction begins on G.P.O.

1815 Pro-Cathedral constructed on Marlborough Street.

1816 Halfpenny Bridge built.

1821 Theatre Royal opens.

1829 'Relief Bill' grants Catholic Emancipation Act.

1835 St Paul's Church constructed on Arran Quay.
1837 Dublin Metropolitan Police formed.
1845 Kingsbridge Station built.
1846 First Bewley's Cafe opens off Dame Street.
1847 Great Famine necessitates opening of soup kitchens throughout city.
1849 Queen Victoria's first visit.
1854 Catholic University founded with Cardinal Newman as rector. Oscar Wilde born.
1858 Fenian movement founded in Dublin and New York.
1859 First issue of *The Irish Times* goes to press.
1865 Fenian newspaper, *The Irish People,* raided, workers arrested. W. B. Yeats born.
1870 Home Rule Movement launched by Isaac Butt.
1871 Remodelling and restoration of Christ Church begins — Winetavern bridge and Chapterhouse built. J. M. Synge born.
1877 National Library of Ireland established.
1881 Land League riots in Dublin. Electric lighting illuminates streets.
1881 British officials murdered in Phoenix Park. James Joyce born.
1903 Women admitted to Trinity.
1904 Abbey Theatre opens.
1909 ITGWU founded, James Larkin secretary.

1914 University College Dublin built
1916 Easter Rising. Martial law decreed. Very extensive destruction of downtown Dublin. Rebels executed at Kilmainham.
1919 Anglo-Irish War starts: old IRA vs. British.
1921 IRA razes Customs House.
1922 Dáil Eireann approves Anglo-Irish Treaty. Civil War begins and Four Courts bombed.
1923 Civil War ends. Yeats wins Nobel Prize for Literature.
1925 George Bernard Shaw wins Nobel Prize for Literature.
1928 Gate and Peacock Theatres open.
1936 First Aer Lingus flight.
1937 New Constitution.
1949 Republic of Ireland established.
1961 RTE begins TV broadcasting.
1966 Nelson Pillar blown up.
1969 Samuel Beckett wins Nobel Prize for Literature.
1972 British Embassy on St Stephen's Green burnt down in aftermath of Bloody Sunday massacre in Derry.
1975 Destruction of Wood Quay begins despite existence of medieval timber structures on site.
1979 Pope addresses one third of entire population in Phoenix Park.
1985 Royal Hospital Kilmainham renovated and opened to public. Anglo-Irish Agreement signed.
1988 Millennium celebrations in Dublin.

For K. K. and other friends from **September 1987**

First published **1988 by** The O'Brien Press, 20 Victoria **Road,** Dublin 6, Ireland.
Copyright © Stephen Conlin
ISBN 0-86278-171-X
HB ISBN 0-86278-174-4
Printed by Brookfield Printing Company Ltd., Blackrock, Co. Dublin

Acknowledgements Roger Stalley (TCD), Edward McParland (TCD), Howard Clarke (UCD), Pat Johnson (Dublin Civic Museum), Pat Wallace (National Museum), Muriel McCarthy (Marsh's Library), Conn Manning and Anne Lynch (Office of Public Works),Siobhán de hÓir (Royal Society of Antiquaries of Ireland), The Keeper of Manuscripts (Trinity College Dublin), Peter Walsh (Guinness Museum), Enda Cunningham (Viking Banquets and Entertainments Ltd), Mr I.R. Gault (Rotunda Hospital), Ms M. Clark (Dublin Corporation City Archives), Thaddeus Breen, Pat Healy, Leo Swan, Sheila Watts, Harold Clarke, Victor Jackson, Mr F.E. Dixon, Mr Cassidy (Pembroke Estate Office), Mrs Maureen Cashman, Jeremy Williams, Patrick Cooke (St Enda's College, Rathfarnham), Pat Brady, Margaret Lynam, Andrzej Wejchert, Seamus McIneaney, Tony O Dálaigh (Royal Hospital Kilmainham), John de Courcy.
The following libraries: Pearse Street, ILAC Centre, Dun Laoghaire, the Irish Architectural Archive, the Royal Society of Antiquaries of Ireland, the Royal Irish Academy, Trinity College Dublin.